Learning to Lasso the Moon

C.R. Andrews

ISBN-13: 978-1517367299
ISBN-10: 1517367298

DEDICATION

This book is dedicated to the woman
who has yet to reveal herself.

The one who offers
something more.
The lasso,
the moon,
and the girl next door.

CONTENTS

C.R. Andrews

FOREWORD

Well here we are. Another few months. Another book. Contained here is my life during the summer of 2015. I was still recovering from the dark stage that I was in while writing *Empty Birds in Broken Pianos* and again my writing had increased to an even more obsessive, frantic pace. The bulk of the material created during this recent journey is contained in here. This time around though, I have omitted dozens of pieces. Partly to cut down on the length of the book and partly because some of it was absolute nonsense. Of course, I've left a lot of random thoughts and nonsense in just to paint a complete picture. The material here is also in chronological order to show the evolution of my emotions and thought process. Although dressed up with some romance and sex, *Heartmeat* was hopeless and *Empty Birds* was a downward spiral. Something different happened during this period of writing though. I was learning from myself as I would brood and spit my venom until I got to the point where it was all out. I began examining myself. Quite simply, I had grown so terribly weary of being angry. I didn't want it anymore. There will always be darkness in me and it will always live in my work. But the time came when it was time to write about the longing, the ache, and the rapture of beautiful things. Of love. So you, my dear readers, thank you for spending this time now with my book in your hands and please enjoy my journey from tales of despair in the bottom of a pit to shameless, cheesy love notes in the park.

<u>these words</u>

these thoughts
these words
they may disturb you
but this is all i have

every word you read
no matter how dark
is the only reason that
you are not
looking at
me displayed
in
a wooden
box.

<u>fool</u>

a man
who trusts you
cannot be trusted

for only a
great fool
or the village idiot
would be so
easily led
by such delicate
promises

i proceed to walk by
and hear them snicker
at the idiot
and the fool,

missed again

another girl
another bottle
another tombstone
another scar
another dead fire
another wish
another dream
another promise
another lost kiss
another miss.

welcome back

that little twitching
in my hands
has returned and
this glass empties
faster and faster
until i can thread a
needle with a spider's silk
i remember this place
this is the muse and
the mistress that
welcomes me back with
loving arms
she cools my tongue and
needs no words
she helps me stumble to
the bed and spin into
blackness before i can
lament the empty side
where you should be.

on the wagon

there is a reason that
nobody ever says

"i used to be an alcoholic"

however you change your life
and regardless of the time
expired it is always

"i am an alcoholic"

you are a former drug addict but
never a former alcoholic

you are either a drunk
or a recovering alcoholic

you are always
on the wagon

never in the middle

there is no such thing as
one drink
or five
there is only oblivion

and if you think otherwise
then you are probably
a drunk like me.

silence

do you hear that?
the silence of it?
turn in to the wind
breathe in
can you smell it now?
someone just died.

no fear

i fear nothing

not a beating
not death
not disease
certainly not the loss
of your love
i can't lose something
that was fabricated
and only existed
between
the last drink
and
the flush of a toilet
my only fear is that this
is how it all ends.

<u>too much</u>

i drink too much
and my hands
shake too much

i eat too much
or not at all

i never sleep
or sleep all day

i cry too much
love too hard
and hate too deep

i've learned too much
i feel too much
and all the wrong ones
are the ones
i crave too much.

i believed you

i believed you
again i believed someone
you say it wasn't malicious
it wasn't your intent
your intent is as worthless
as piss
again i am a chapter
not even a chapter but
a footnote
a phase
a fleeting fantasy
something you secretly
spit into a napkin and
feed to a hungry dog under
the table while you smile
as if you truly
loved the meal

you are the most dangerous
and surreptitious whore.

how does it feel?

how do you lead this life?
is it worth it?
how does it feel with yet
another man who doesn't even
want to kiss you?
drink that bottle
spread your legs
go ahead and let these men
treat you exactly
how you feel
and as your tears continue
to fall
i will continue
to say
goodbye.

nothing special

just remember
when you think you are special
something is going to hit you
right in the nose and remind you
that you are no different
than anyone else who tried to
swim these waters
you are recycled from the scrap heap
you are the pieces of other men
you inspire nothing
you are not a unique and
beautiful flower
that thing you see in the mirror
is exactly what they all see.

under a rock

it is time to
go back
beneath the stone
that remains
unturned
for not one
wished it
to be lifted
to begin with.

guilty

it is only
the truly guilty
and the wicked
that can
sleep
soundly
for they feel
neither wicked
nor
guilty.

<u>et tu?</u>

in the end
it will always be
the one you thought you
could trust the most
the only one in the
crowd that you truly loved
Judas
and Brutus
wrapped
up in the package of a
tight little body and
an alluring smile
realizing they pulled the
strings of your demise
all along
and i have been debased
just as much as
the heart
i thought was true.

rock bottom

i'm the guy you
wake up next to
that makes you
question
how you ever
managed
to sink so low.

i was the one

i was the one who
didn't care where
you had been
or
about the men that
had you before me
i was the one who
looked
into your eyes instead of
just bending you over
i was the one who
was
just as thrilled by your
kiss as i was by
your open legs
i was the one who
adored you and
i was the only one
that you pushed away.

i'm better

i was so enamored
so infatuated with you
since that first night
and though i knew
i would never make it
past your eyes
i felt as if my mouth
was already on yours
my fingers had already
slid down between
abandoned thighs
and we both know that
the fantasy of these
scarred hands and
the reality of
my desperate words
in your ear will always
make you cum harder
than any
one night stand.

<u>time heals all</u>

now begins another length of time
where each night
i will relive that first night
the subsequent nights
and the final night
all the things said and unsaid
declarations that brought me
back to life and then the great
unveiling of how false it
all really was
a new lullaby of
i forgive you
i do not forgive you
i forgive you
i do not forgive you. . .

junkyard

my skin is
a pale junkyard
of hair and
faded tattoos
an abandoned battlefield
of burned and flayed skin
and still active land mines
arms to once be
cast in bronze
and legs that
ran like a gazelle
are now stiff vines
and tree trunks
but somewhere
in all of this mess
someone will see the reflection
of what i used to be
someone beautiful
and clean
someone not quite so ugly
not quite ruined
and
only mostly dead.

condition 1

my mouth open as
the brushed nickel
rests on my tongue
the metal and the
fresh oil is
surprisingly sweet
i glance around for
a last look at some pictures
in a frame
at the room that
i'll be found in
click clack
i flash back to
the safety rules
condition 1
hammer back
safety off
round in chamber
finger on trigger
then a meow
a purr
soft fur nudging my leg
big bewildered eyes staring
a paw slowly reaching
with a gentle pat on
my chin
back to
condition 4
it's ok buddy
i won't leave you all alone.

turning to stone

she was youth and freedom
he was old and rigid
she was a wood nymph
a gazelle
he was a tired satyr
she was a sprite pixie
he was a weary knight
she was paving a
path of glitter
he was covering it
with dirt
she was the prize
he never caught and
then he finally
turned to stone.

not here

you're not here
you
are not here

my words
your words
mean nothing

you're not here
you
are not here

and i watch you
disappear.

<u>always here</u>

as i look around at
all the places in
my house where
you sat
where you laughed
all of the places
your clothes fell
the pillows where
you once laid your head
it has already been
nearly a year since
this room echoed with
your voice

i was so sure that
you were gone

but there you are
but here you are

i am alone
and i am not alone.

<u>crazy cat guy</u>

don't look for
a deeper meaning
i'm not
intense
or intelligent
i'm not
insightful
i know
nothing
about women
i know less than
you do about
pretty much
everything
i'm just some old guy
wearing socks with sandals
scratching his ass
in a house with
too many cats.

<u>fuckery</u>

i could say we fought
the good fight
i could say that we tried
but we killed it
from the first spark
we gave everyone else control
but ultimately this
is on us

he said

she said

i did

you did

i heard this

i heard that

absorbing every detail
except for the truth
perhaps that is all easier
than the truth
oh what a
convoluted
pile of
fuckery
we have created.

x marks the spot

it is strange that i can
manage to attract women
with what i have
on the surface
considering
that it isn't much
of a surface

somehow i've managed
to create an image
that inspires wanting
a manufactured aura that
promises there is
something deeper
under the surface
something beautiful

but when i let them
crack the shell
the disappointment
comes

they find no
treasure within and
in a single moment
the surface and
the soul
are equally
repulsive.

<u>where are you?</u>

it is the middle of the night
and i don't know why
i should be so drunk
and so alone
i don't know why we are
not either drunk and
laughing together
or passed out together
i don't know why your
face is not resting
against me
i don't know why i am
not feeling you
on me right now
your leg should be
draped over mine
i should be
stroking your hair
i should be
hearing your voice
where are you lover?

stop

i have been as
thinly veiled
as naked flesh
it has always been there
for the world to see
so let's stop making
avoidance appear accidental
let's stop pretending that
things are so complicated
let's stop being liars
let's stop pretending our
lives are so busy
stop the ride
stop the dance
just stop.

disclaimer

i don't
look back anymore
and question if
i was
really in love
it's quite a silly thing actually
i don't care what
you turned out to be
i don't care if
i was fooled
i don't need a
backdated disclaimer
make no mistake
it was love
and i will never regret that
i offered you
everything
nor
that it was refused.

<u>you didn't want it</u>

i already offered it
this is a package deal baby
you didn't want it
you wanted
the pretty things
the brightest and
the ripest fruit
not the stem or the seed
and certainly not the root
did you really think
you were the
only girl in town?

<u>what a shame</u>

another day ended
another week passed
the clock seemed
slow enough

but then one day
i was beating the dust
from the pillow
the cats had long been dead
the water heater had rusted out
the walls were nicotine yellow
i went back to sleep and
continued to wait for you

the next morning a stranger
saw my name in the paper
and thought

"so young what a shame"
then carried on with his day.

<u>free</u>

i forgive you
is that what you need?
i forgive you
that does not mean
i can see you
that does not mean
i can hear your voice
but like Pilate
i wash my hands
of my blood and yours
because i won't let this
hate destroy me
i won't make you the
victim of these words
any longer
i loved you then
i love you still
but i set us both free.

eventually

eventually
this will all
just dry up
i'm not diverse
i have a limited scope
of love
lips
and pussy
and the searching for it
kisses here
fingers there
playthings and
unrequited
fraudulent love
fireworks and fairytales
love at first sight and
all things believed by
children who believe they
can really come true.

nobody left

so there i sat
barren
alone
naked and bare as
the pages before me
there is no one
in my head
my breathing and
my heartbeat
have slowed
all of these lovelies were
merely smoke that
has since cleared
and there is simply
nobody left to
write for.

<u>poof</u>

and just
like
that
all of
my
words
had
gone.

unnecessary virtue

who is the asshole that
came up with the idea
that learning to be alone
was a necessary virtue?
whoever you are
go suck a bag of dicks
cuntface.

stronger

i'm growing stronger
you made me stronger
i feel fortunate that
i'm turning you
over to the next
i always thought that
those women were
breaking me down
but they are
tightening my skin
sharpening my vision
my teeth and my nails
can tear through stone
you gave me control
over every other woman
that will cross my path.

dead poets

stop being clever
stop forcing metaphors
you don't have to say that
everything affects your soul
to show that
something touched you
say what you mean
if you're lucky
you can write
just as shitty as me
Bukowski
Neruda
Cummings
Lorca
are all dead
use your language
not theirs
remember
we are the next dead poets.

Hank

do you want to know why
i love Bukowski?
it isn't because of his genius
it is because of those pieces he wrote
that are complete shit
it is all building to something
you are watching the
creative mind unfold
he is working things out
he is not giving a fuck
he makes you feel like you could
write the same way
then you turn to that page
and realize why he is a writer
and you are not.

more Hank

why else do i love Bukowski?
because he was a beast
he was hideous
i grew up as the
ugly fat kid with bad skin
the shunned one and
the one that the girls laughed at
were repulsed by
and now i'm a dirty old man
with strong arms and a big belly
but i'm coming into a time
where it doesn't matter
women don't see the ugliness
that i see
there are women out there
that don't see the beast
they just see me.

remember when?

do you remember when
i was so fat that you couldn't
even fit your little
arms around me?

do you remember when
i was so thin that
i was even more
fragile than you?

do you remember
the times when
we both
stopped breathing?

do you remember the
months that i
fed and bathed you?

do you remember the
nights you helped
me to bed?

just remember that
our strength is
and was
the stuff of legends.

everything is new

a muse isn't
always someone
that you write about
she makes you
see everything
everything around you
you taste things differently
you smell new scents
she unlocks a passion
a passion for life
a passion for her
and a passion for
all of the things
around you
she will make you feel
all of the places that
make you tremble
she will make you see
the beauty in life
if you are foolish enough
if you are truly stupid
you will try to own her
silly boy
she was never
yours to keep.

drowning

i can't save you
if you have
already made up
your mind
to simply fill up
your lungs
and drown.

i can't be him

i can't be those men
you have loved
i can't be the men
who have loved you
and i can't be the man
who has you
but i will still be here
with fading fingerprints
and vacant hands
pushing this pencil
just fighting to be
a part of
the woman who
should have loved me.

<u>i am flawed</u>

i am well aware that
i am flawed

i am well aware that
with me
there is
a lot of work that
needs to be done

but there is one thing
that i know how to do

i know how to love

i know how to make you
the only one

you just had to say the word

you could have called down
the thunder

you could have drowned the
world around us

why didn't you?

i'm retired

i am done chasing women
the ones that don't know
what they want
the ones that don't know
what they want from me

i am done chasing girls
with the daddy issues
the ones with fleeting needs
and the ones that haven't
figured out a damn thing in life

i am done chasing possibilities
i am done chasing the
promise of something
i am the retired hunter
it is time for someone to
make me the prey.

<u>the letter</u>

i pulled your letter out
of its resting place
it is all that
i have left of you
it was actually all
that i ever had
i held the crease
against my nose and
mouth and tried to
breathe in
what was left
perhaps i even
kissed it
it just smells like
blank paper now
yet i still smell you
on the pages as if
you were really here
i carry that scent
to the kitchen
to the sofa
to the warm breeze
in the window
it mixes with the smell of
cigarettes and freshly cut grass
and i carry it to the pillow
next to mine
and in the morning
it is still there.

all of them

i will love them all
the unavailable
the unattainable
the unrealistic
the ones who already have
more than i can offer
more than i could ever be
the ones either unloved or
in the arms of beautiful men
oceans away or
the girl next door
and i will keep believing that
i am the man
who can change their life.

mindfuck

i will fuck your mind
i will fuck your body
i will fuck the past
right out of you
i will fuck you a new future
i will fuck you back
to your virginity
i will make you feel both
violated and adored
then i will do it
all again and
i will fuck you into
a new kind of love.

<u>we are writers</u>

let us never forget that
we are writers
we don't compromise
we feel and fuck and
cry more than anyone and
sometimes we drink more
than a Kennedy at an open bar

we won't let crocodiles tell
us how we should
express ourselves and
we won't beg you to
tell us our work is
worth something

we don't need
anything but a
pencil.

<u>i don't care</u>

at one time
i never cared
what was going on in
a woman's head
as long as she was
attractive and eager
but somehow
as i got older and
less attractive
the girls got younger
more attractive
and more frequent
but less appealing

the physical act of fucking
is pretty dull by itself

if you don't want me in
your mind then why do i
give a damn what is
between your legs?

hidden away

you might not want to
show me off
you might not want to
walk down the street with me
you might not want
pictures with me
you won't want to
marry me
you won't want to
live under my roof
you won't tell your friends
about me
you can be ashamed
i would be too
but as long as we can
have these moments in the dark
i'll keep being the one
you would never fight for.

<u>over 40</u>

when you are over 40 you start
hurting in the strangest places
places that have nothing to do
with the issues you already know of
why the fuck does my 3rd toe
suddenly feel like it is being chewed on?
what the fuck is this spot on my face?
why do i feel like i just cracked a rib while
i took a bite of a sandwich?
why are those damn kids outside so loud?
who in the actual fuck are these people
on the grammy awards?
when did we phase out instruments, singing,
and songwriting?
Ooh, is my oatmeal ready?

last cigarette

one more cigarette and
one more drink
just a few more minutes
of staring out of
the kitchen window
and thinking about the ways that
i keep trying
all the wrong hearts that
i dip my finger in and
begin to stir
and i wonder if i have
made it out to
the other side
why so many are
still afraid to love.

<u>the attic</u>

there is a dusty little place
behind my heart and
there is still a little room
left for you if
you can wade through
the cigarette butts
and razors
the empty bottles and
the tumbleweeds
the broken bones
piles of scars
and the faded memories

if you can make that journey
then that small pure corner
is yours to fill
but
hurry
please hurry
because it is filling up fast
and then this door
will close forever.

delicate lunatic

she is hard to describe
she is a delicate lunatic
imagine a love child born from
Manson
Jennifer Tilly
and a Smurf
then cover her in tattoos and
give her a big knife
on an average night she
stitches up her own
skull with piano wire before
crawling into bed
like a child and wrapping
dangerous legs around
me so softly
clinging with koala bear cuddles
and cooing softly
against my chest.

<u>army ants</u>

show me the place
inside of you
where the insects crawl
the part of you
that is being
eaten away
something
always digging
something
always screaming
the tunnels in your brain
where
they are marching
always marching
the spaces between the ink
the inches of skin that are
still free from pain
those spaces i will kiss and
trace letters with
my old fingers and
remind you that
you are
still alive.

danger

she was as subtle as
a chainsaw being
rammed through a
pane of wire-mesh
safety glass
but she knew how to
be as gentle and as
soft as moonlight
and i didn't know
which part of her
that i needed more.

a fitting end

i stood here
while the arena fell
when the reckoning came
i should have joined the mob
but i've dropped my torch
into the fountain and
i've put the pitchfork away
i've received your act
of contrition
and it is punishment enough
for you to live every day
knowing that you cut down
the one man who truly loved you.

<u>born again</u>

i see you found Jesus

fuck

that poor bastard

wish i could have
warned him about you.

<u>hands</u>

i've always looked younger
than i am.
i've been lucky that way
people would say
"you don't look 30"
"you don't look 40"
the thing is that
people look at my face
and not at my hands
they have aged 20 years
in the last two
that is where time catches you
one too many conflicts
with doors and walls
and windows
too much time fixing things
that are broken
a hundred years' worth of
caressing the wrong women
and a hundred more reaching
out to them.

half measures

i don't need your half measures

the temptations
the promise of your skin

i have no time for
a fleeting heart

i need you on a rooftop
bare bodied and
screaming my name
until it rends open the sky
and covers us in
hail and snow and rain
until Venus and Mars
come crashing down
and every star is
drawn and quartered from
your yearning siren song
and it consumes us in
a pyre of faith and flesh
then
my beauty
i need you to
jump.

let me write for you

let me write about you again
now that
my head is clear
now that
the truth is out
just tell me
that you
want it again
and i will press this
pencil between my
fingers until they
fucking bleed for you.

word vomit

i've got more words for you
they are in here somewhere
i have more words
they will come to me
any minute now
something perfect to
describe you
it's on the tip of my tongue
wait i've got it
oh sorry that was
just me throwing up
a little in my mouth.

moments of joy

i've given up on finding
the one
that perfect fit
it isn't so sad a thing
it is better to know that
it is too late before
time does it for you
i will look for those
small moments of joy
in between the nights
and the days before death
who will join me?

pirouettes

it gets a little easier
every time they
change their mind
each time they
say goodbye
all the times i've
watched
their little feet
doing pirouettes
on all those dimes
spin and twirl little girl
because i've
already disappeared
there is another
there is always another
and i am too close
to death to
keep chasing my tail.

<u>it's that simple</u>

it all comes down to this
you are just a woman
i am just a man

we are false
and flawed

now that the fog of war
has cleared
what are you prepared to do?

because just as
i always was
i am right here waiting
for you.

<u>revenge</u>

i'm going to
hunt down
and
snap the neck
of every man
who ever
damaged you
for ruining
the possibility
of
us.

go to him

once
i was falling in
love with you
perhaps a reckless love
a foolish irrational love
but when am i allowed
to love?

when is it permitted and
not misguided lust?
can we love
without touch?
without voices?
is it still love when it is
unrequited?
is it selfish that i hate
your love being for another?
should i not wish you happiness?

go my love
go to him
goodbye

for when you open your
eyes here there is nothing
but white noise and
things just a bit too far
from peace.

<u>big bad wolf</u>

she skips and wanders
in half-shrouded beauty
along paths paved for her
toes to glide
velvet moonlight skin
and the reddest of tresses
linger on every flower
and bird's song that
pays witness to her
as she passes
forever covered with
her scent and her grace
a beauty such as this
even the hungriest of wolves
would not dare to approach.

<u>one speed</u>

with women
i have one speed
all in
pedal to the floor
reckless
stupid
jumping without a net
sappy poems and love notes
breakfast in bed
obsessive fawning
shameless declarations
and idealized pedestals
and while they pine over
searching for exactly this
i sit in solitude
chipping at marble
waiting to be discovered.

a thousand times

you cannot leave
this world
though we have
parted
you were and will
always be my world

you will come
out of the darkness

i am always here

no longer joined
in holy union but
i have not forgotten
my vows
and
i will
remain true to them
even if it ruins me

we could not
remain together
but i will still love you

a thousand times
i love you.

your eyes are bigger than your stomach

i am something that
you think you want
that big fattening piece of
cheesecake with the little
freshly shaved
white chocolate bits
and the blueberry drizzle that
keeps passing you by on the
dessert cart
you don't need it but
you are convinced you
can't leave
without a taste
but then
you end up
full of
regret
and covered in
the scent
of sex and shame.

<u>my voice</u>

do you feel that?
the tightness in your chest
the urge to shift your legs
the inexplicable reason
that you need to flip your hair
and slowly run your
fingers through it
the reason that strap falls
off of your shoulder
just slightly
the reason you curl your
toes against the sofa cushion
and smile and brush your
fingertips
along your
collarbone

that is the sound of
my voice.

unfinished thoughts

what is it that
lingered
on your lips?
a question?
an observation?
as the words never formed
and crept back
behind your
seastorm eyes
did they become
a dream?
as your long fragile
eyelashes fluttered
did you hear the
true answer or
just dream of
what you wanted
it to be?

<u>single life</u>

this is the life
the freedom of single life

living how i want

breakfast from the gas station
lunch from the 7-11
a bottle for dinner while
eating toast over the sink

okay
in my head it didn't sound
that pathetic.

blue button eyes

that girl with the blue button eyes
and the colorful sleeves
oh how she loves her man
the man who won't believe
that he is beautiful
but he will learn
because of her

she loves his words and
his face and hands
she sees not a single flaw
she sees nothing but gold

because of her
because of him
i will continue to believe
there is a woman who can
see me with
eyes like hers.

closer

closer
closer still to
that day
the day when
you
no longer matter
when you
are a ghost
redacted from
every story
the day that
she comes along
the day
our eyes meet
and i hear a voice that
drowns yours
to
less
than a whisper
i can almost
smell her hair
and she is glorious.

someone to watch over you

how does that
old song go?
i'm not a man that
most girls
think of as handsome
but i might carry the key
i'll watch over you
the nights will finally
feel safe
your little head
can rest
forget what the magazines and
the fairytales have told you
about Prince Charming
because sometimes
your savior
and your Lancelot
can be a beast like me.

something more

i want someone to
tolerate my bad habits
but i also want someone
to tame them
someone i put
my lips on
before a bottle
someone who will
kiss me and
make me inhale
their breath instead of
these filthy cancer sticks
someone who doesn't care
about the size of my belly
but makes me want to
get rid of it
someone who settles
for what i am but
makes me want to
be so much more.

silly bitch

i know i have already met you
you're right there
i can feel it
you will be the reason that
i take my last drink
the reason i stop sucking down
plumes of cigarette smoke
the reason i drop 20 pounds
the one who gets me to
bed before 11:00
the one whose hair i'm
brushing away from my face
in the morning
i'm too weary to guess
so take a step forward
just betray all this mystery
with a kiss

kiss me you silly bitch.

<u>finally there</u>

this is where your hands belong
now that you feel mine on you
everything is falling into place
i think it is time that we
end this dance
this night we thought
would never come is
here now
i can finally feel
that taut back
and my fingers
gliding across those ribs
the delicious caverns
of your clavicle
the spun golden straw
of your hair
the throbbing pulse in
your long neck
and the unnatural
outline of
your lips.

<u>come away</u>

come away
run away with me
be my lover
be the brutal waves of lust
be the reason ink and fingers bleed
be my childhood fantasies of
movie stars and centerfolds
be my muse
be my doll
my whore and
my princess
be my girl
be my wife
be the one that shatters
already shattered pieces
be the one to
go the distance
be the one stronger
than me

come away
run away
and be the one
that ends the darkness.

my imaginary wife

i dreamed a dream that
you were my wife
no
you did not leave him for me
it was simply
a life that was always
you and i
nights of
slow dancing
to Debussy
mornings of
scrambled eggs
and Mozart
not a new life but
a rewritten life
your children
were our children
and in this life you loved me
and you were free to
let me love you
and we loved
until the gods wept.

who are you?

we will have our time
i know it is coming soon
i will finally feel your flesh
warm and wet and new
the only thing
standing between us
is that i don't know
your name
what you look like
or where you
are in this world.

<u>imminent</u>

when she finally
kills me
it won't be softly
it will be a loud
and
excruciating
death.

<u>i promise</u>

i promise i won't
i won't fall in love with you
i will never ask for more
i promise i won't make
your face into an altar
i won't make your mouth and
your breath my reason
for living
i will not fall in love with you
i promise i won't look at
your body as if it has
rewritten my past
i won't make your eyes into
chariots of saviors
i promise i wont
i wont
i promise you
i wont love you
i promise
i love you.

John Stamos

growing up
i always wanted to be
one of those ridiculously
handsome men
tall and striking
with the piercing blue eyes
of Paul Newman
broad shoulders like
Christopher Reeve
a voice like
Gregory Peck
the chiseled jaw and
cheekbones like
Rick Springfield and
John Stamos
now 25 years later
i have to deal with
Hugh Jackman
Chris Hemsworth
and
wait
why the fuck is
John Stamos still around?

imperfections

give me a woman
with some flaws
maybe some mommy stripes
or a head a little too big for
her skinny neck
thighs too close together or
too far apart
imperfect teeth that
give her lips a little shape
that little pudge
below her belly button
hips too wide or hips that
look like a famine victim
tits too big or flat as a board
too prudish or too crude
tattoos and acne scars and
anything that shows she has
lived outside of what
we think is beautiful
where it never matters what our eyes
have been conditioned to see
only how our bodies feel
in each other's hands.

<u>i know it when i see it</u>

i may have
no idea
what poetry is but
i know it
when i see it

no

this is not it.

cemetery

you can damn me for
every fleeting glance
every wink and a smile
you can fume over
any compliment that
comes my way
but at the end of the day
just remember that you
always go home to him
while my bed
is still a cemetery.

say it again

say it again
say the words
any words at all
anything that allows me
to hear that voice
anything that lets me
hear that immaculate
mouth form words
words formed for me
and lips created to
form to mine.

right here

read to me again love
tell me a story
a story of the love
we both search for
a story that quite possibly
is being written
right here
in this bed.

<u>destroy him</u>

i want to be the one
you use to break
another man's heart
to crush the dream of
what he thought was his
where he screams out
"why
him?"
and then you smugly
list the reasons
one by one
and watch
him
crumble.

<u>sweat</u>

how are you going to
tell him that
all those poems you
wrote
were written
while
my sweat
was still drying
on
your back?

show me

show me your shoulder
show me your outstretched neck
expose your throat
and your bones
let me see you stripped down
the skin behind the words
broken down and bare
let my fingertips and
my voice show you that
your ethereal beauty matches
your aesthetic perfection
that every word i speak
is urged by your existence
say it
say yes
and do it tonight.

tell me

tell me
tell me you're mine
tell me
tell me what he did
then tell me
tell me where he is
unleash me
release the lion
and let me show you
what i am
really capable of.

Fred

there is a tiny spider who
has made a home at the corner of
my kitchen window sill

it has been about 4 weeks now

i really need to clean this part of
the window but he isn't hurting anyone
i named him Fred

Fred is just looking for his
little place in the world like me
i talk to Fred sometimes

sometimes Fred talks back

i have clearly lost my mind.

at your feet

you are far more
than you think
we all think that we
aren't enough
that the answer is
to give more
instead of
finding the person
that we are enough for

never doubt
and never
marginalize
the wonder that you are
never compromise
it is out there
and if this old fool can
see it
then somewhere
there is an army just waiting
to kneel
at your pale feet.

Rach's 3rd

we went to the symphony
you were dressed in all black
with that choker around your throat
it was Rachmaninoff's 3rd
he was no Van Cliburn but
damn that kid could play
i watched you react all night
crossing and uncrossing your legs
your hands adjusting your dress
and not so subtly caressing
your thighs as you smoothed
out the fabric

i put my hand on your leg
and you squeezed it as
we both absorbed the
fingers caressing the keys
then stroking them
then pounding them
all mimicking what we
both knew would happen
when i had you alone

i knew what this did to you
you knew what this did to me
you slowly looked at me
i slowly turned to you
as the crescendo grew your
small chest rose and fell
your lips quivered as you
exhaled and slowly swallowed

you smiled and this night had
already become what we
always thought it would be

we didn't say a word
after the final note
not on the way to the car
or on the trip home
we wanted nothing to
break this moment
you didn't make a sound
until we were home and
i unzipped your dress and
let it fall to the floor
then it was time to
play you

i caressed you like Chopin
i stripped you down to
nothing like Beethoven
and i ravaged you like Brahms
and that night
in that room
i made your body timeless

the dollhouse

back in your house
little dollie
i'm done playing
with you today

back to your cage
your tea parties
and paper mache' bed

in my evening
and your morning
i'll open the curtains
and take you out
of the dollhouse
to play with you
and pull your
strings
once again.

take it all

take all of my words and
every single kiss
let them swim through
your hair and
trickle down your
soft flesh
your naked abandoned
shoulders
the bitter and
the weary inches of
your body
be calmed and
place them beneath your
pillow where you lay your
precious breath
i wish for you
generous dreams
pillars of perfect ideals
for you
the chosen manifestation of
the purest beauty
o how deserving is thee.

<u>indefinable</u>

the impossibility of
comparing or
defining
your beauty
is what drives
lesser poets
like me
into
complete
madness.

properly kissed

when is
the last time
you were properly kissed?
when it wasn't foreplay and
the moment was only about the kiss?
when there were no bodies but only lips?
come here lover and close your eyes
that time is now.

i'm taking over

even reserved
and restrained
her face is a smile
she will hide it
coy and demure
but the corners of
her mouth
are curling
i'm breaking through
i know her hands begin to
wander down her
body
a little more
each time she
hears my voice
those thighs ease open
just a little wider
fingers that she wishes were mine
disappear
and only knuckles
remain grinding quietly
as the cuckold beside her
sleeps soundly.

the girl next door

she has been burning you
down for years
this firewoman
the Bettie Page of suburban legend
the silhouette that graced
B-52s and Zippo lighters
the perfect legs on billboards
glowing in the spotlights above
the Kennedy expressway that
caused the 20 car pileup
and she's still got it
she's a woman
not some little girl
she is out of the cellar
and babe
she's gonna leave you.

it's all a joke
<u></u>

someone needs to invent
something
new
or discover something
new

unexplained wonders
that came from
man or nature

because
the Sphinx is a Taco Bell
the Parthenon is a McDonald's
the Grand Canyon is a cliché
and walking on the moon
has become a joke
ever since
i ran my fingers though
your hair.

the little things

it's the little things
that's where you missed
the mark

you bought her a car
but i read her writing
and she reads mine

you turned over in bed
right next to her
but she knows i am
longing for her to make
mine a little less empty

i listen to her stories
i watch her dance
i covet her smile
i play with her hair

and i kiss her every time
like we just met.

<u>what the hell are we doing?</u>

i have no idea
what we are doing
why we are doing it
what can happen
what to expect
and what goes through
this simple mind
but here i am
which one of us will
eat the other alive?

not a moment wasted

any thoughts i could have of
a woman are hers
the dark fantasies of 9 ½ Weeks
and g-rated moments of
Lady and the Tramp
she is the Norman Rockwell moments
of my childhood and the bandages
for nights of self-destruction
any day i do not make her smile
is a wasted day
any night she does not need my touch
is a wasted night
and any moment not scrolling of
her beauty is one where i continue
to wither.

<u>she was a song</u>

i could see her skin dance
electric flesh leaping from
fingertip to fingertip
uttering little pieces of my name
each time interrupted as my
hand explored another inch
another treasure
she was liquid silk in my hands
living
languid
lascivious
silk
twisting writhing grinding
i made her body into a song that
no other lesser man could sing again.

awestruck

i am in awe with every
glimpse of her
i should learn to sculpt or
paint or make something more
than words
because there are none
none to make her believe
none to pull her in
none to prevent adoration from
being met with apoplectic rage
and nobody
to cut me down
when my imminent
swing
from the gallows comes.

<u>all for you</u>

for you
i would be the fool

i would
scorch my feathers
in the sun

i would
dig my own grave
as you blew me kisses

i would
blind myself to
other beauty

i would
wait silent and
shivering at the bottom
of a well

i would
pave undiscovered
roads for your feet

i would destroy myself
i would shame myself
burn the world
challenge the gods
and be your champion.

pictures

i saw a picture of you
and i hated you
i hated that somebody
made you exist to
torment me
like you were a reminder of
trees too tall to climb and
rivers too unpredictable to swim
of stars that have been dead for
millions of years before i could
reach them
and i only wish i could have
gotten there faster to be
burned alive before i
could indulge in your beauty.

dead space

i pray to a god that
i don't believe in
i curse at nonexistent evils
there must be someone
to blame
somebody out there is
responsible for
keeping you from me
i damned the stars and
debased the moon
attempting to make this
space between us
a little smaller
i nursed hummingbirds and
bred colonies of
butterflies to create
some sort of
karma and grace
but i still wake
every day surrounded by
the desperate spaces that
can only be
filled by you.

deeper

i need you to feel this need
that crawls inside my body
not those typical places like
the heart and the soul
they are tired of being written about
they are insignificant in your presence

think
deeper

deeper than flesh
deeper than the heart
that need that is deep down in
the marrow of my bones
the immolation of my blood
the stirring of locusts and
bluebirds in my brain
let me touch you just once
do you feel it now?

her scars

i learned every
scar on her body
i heard the story
behind each one
i kissed them
i memorized them
and instead of
kissing them away
i kissed them deeper
into her and made
each one mine.

no more words

let me taste those breaths
in between sentences
let me kiss you in that
little space where you pause
instead of searching
for the next thing to say

just let me kiss you

let me make you forget
what you were about to say
let my kiss be
the next thing you
need on those lips

no more words
just my lips on yours.

any kind of touch

just tell me i will touch you
let me know that just once
we can both fool ourselves
just that one touch
any sort of skin on skin
hand in hand
cheek to cheek
lips to lips
even so slight as just that
final moment when we part
taking a little too long
to say goodnight
something
anything that makes this
not seem like madness.

run aground

i've memorized your face
certain parts of your body
i've filled in the pieces
i've never seen
those taunting areas of you
that i have touched with these fingers
like bold cartographers of mystery
tracing out the land between your
collarbone and your ribs
from your hip bones across
every curve down to your ankles
i may never explore that land
the islands of flesh made
for greater men
but i know that you can still
feel me crawling
upon the shore.

i'll never stop

i'll never stop wanting to
make you smile
until your
cheeks hurt
i'll never stop infuriating you
with adoration just so
i can see you scowl and
crinkle your nose at me
i'll never stop making
you blush or
tire of your
fake pouting
and i will never lose the
flutter in my chest as if
the bottle just stopped
spinning and pointed
across from me at
the prettiest girl in school.

a new life

if you were mine
it would be the life
you were always meant to lead
tell me how much of your life
that you want to change
and
i will baptize you into
a new life
in a new world
we can replace your childhood
we can change the senior prom
we can erase a loveless marriage
you would be surprised
how much
i can change
with my voice against your ear
and my hands upon your body.

<u>keep playing</u>

if i told you that
your face is the beauty
i've searched every
monument and
work of art for
you won't believe it but
you would still
make me say it

if i tell you that your
body is an opus not
worthy of my fingers
you would smash them
against this piano but
ask me to keep
playing

if i said i loved your
heart it would be the
greatest insult
of all

and if it all frustrates
you this much then
imagine how it feels to
be the man who
will never touch you.

do the wrong thing

i want you to say all the wrong things
do all the wrong things
let them see us
making all the wrong choices
let us be the ones that are
disowned by friends and
family and society
let us be the ones meant to fail
let the prince eat poisoned apples
let sleeping beauty burn in her bed
and we will ride off into
the broken skyline of a world
who played it safe.

all the bad things

i want the
worst parts of you
the ones you bury
the ones you try to
throw away
the ones that
make you drink
and pop pills
and make you
wake up screaming
the things you see in
the mirror that
make you cringe
give them all to me
i will make each one
insignificant
and the only thing
left behind
will be your beauty.

she'll never know

she'll never know what it is
that she does to me
she'll never know how the sight
of her makes me grind my
teeth and clench my fist
until my nails cut into my palm
how imagining her scent and her
kiss makes me
kick at the blankets
and twist and shudder

how without her voice in my ear
i never again want to hear music
or birds chirping or cats purring
until she is here

she'll never know
she cannot know.

every love song

she became every love song
The Righteous Brothers and
The Beatles
Smokey Robinson and
the wonderful ridiculousness
of Tom Jones
but she was also Otis Redding's plane
Janis Joplin's Southern Comfort
the bullets through Lennon's heart
and Kurt Cobain's shotgun
but just as all of them
her beauty was eternal
and even in the event of
the death of this love
we will remember.

all of it

you deserve it all
no
not the jewels and
cars and
trips to the salon
the other things
the little things
handwritten love letters
stupid pictures from
a photo booth
a promise ring made
from a twist-tie
a plastic flower in
your hair
souvenir snow globes and
your initials
carved into a tree
hanging pictures together and
warm brownies covered with
gold medal ribbon ice cream
and a man who works for
nothing more than
just to make you
smile.

<u>when i see you again</u>

when i see you again
should we pretend
nothing has changed?
just how deeply should
we bury this?
shall it be as deep
as our scars and
our memories?
let us have just one night in
our lives where we
hide nothing
let us be honest about
just one thing
that you and i both know
where our mouths belong.

<u>what ifs</u>

and what if we were to fall in love?
would you leave him?
would you want me to ask you to?
and what if i did ask you?
would you come running to me with
nothing but a suitcase and a smile?
or are you simply too afraid that
things could never be as beautiful as
they are living in longing for
the man that you need?

please don't feed the animals

tread lightly boy
you cannot catch this
if you catch it
you cannot keep it
there is no bait for
you to lay to lure her
just admire her
from a distance
keep quiet
not because you will
scare her off but because if
you get her attention
she will devour you as
your legs keep kicking and
your lungs fill up with
thick sticky idiot blood.

Wacker Drive

time is winding down
i only have so many
years left in me
let at least
some of that time
be with you
or even just one night to
kiss the fuck out of you
in the backseat
of a Cadillac on
lower Wacker Drive.

aching

this is the worst kind of
ache
the one that
drink won't drown
the one that sleep won't
comfort
the ache that can't be
approached with
reason
a resolution that
won't be reached with
rational thought
it is useless and
impossible
but she calms it just by
letting me write these
words.

another kind of place

there is
another place
another world
where
you and i are lovers
there is no death in
this world
there are
no barriers
this is
our world
it only rains for
our garden and
for our moments of
drinking tea on
the porch
it is everything that
we want it to be
and in
this world
everybody knows
that you are mine.

nothing compares

there are too many poems
too many words about
kisses
about lips
but Cummings never saw
these lips of hers
Keats died before women
like her were created
Byron wouldn't know what
to say about her mouth
and Yeats is fidgeting
in his grave
at the sound of
those lips parting
against mine.

<u>that face</u>

that face
the one on the pillow next
to mine that has me
smiling before i even wake

that face
the one i keep in my wallet to
show people and say
that's my girl

that face
the one that looks at me as
we walk hand in hand and
tells everyone
this is my man

that face
the one that makes me
hate turning off the lamp on
the bedside table at night

and if i already feel this way now
i cannot fathom how it will be
when i have actually fallen in
love with her.

again

once again
i will
crawl into the sheets
and this pillow will
become you
i'll hold it a little too tightly
i'll say your name
i'll hear you saying mine
and i must live this night
again
and again.

petals

hands off of the display
little boy
this is reserved for
a man
a man who
knows more than how to
just moisten the petals and
doesn't just lunge into
the bud and waste and
smear the pollen
you must notice the edges
the shape and the color
inhale and taste from
the stem to the pistil
let the goddess cover you
and envelop you
savor it tonight and
every night for
she has chosen you.

<u>still waiting</u>

i waited tonight
for the moon and stars
to unite us
but they were shrouded in
the same sky that we share
the same sky that
keeps you from me
the clean night air that
collapses my lungs and
my kisses that drift into
oblivion never to even once
find your lips.

<u>one more poem</u>

here is a poem for you to read
once you are old
and alone like me
and a lullaby
for when
even that time becomes
a fragment of the past
tell yourself you
went for it all
you didn't win but
you touched somebody
somewhere
and if you are one of
the lucky ones
there will be a single
stranger
to lay a flower
on your grave.

Printed in Great Britain
by Amazon.co.uk, Ltd.,
Marston Gate.